YOUNG SCIENTIST CONCEPTS & PROJECTS

# ASTRONOMY

R O B I N   K E R R O D

Gareth Stevens Publishing
**MILWAUKEE**

The original publishers would like to thank Nicholas Lie and Fabian Akinola, Nichola Barnard, Jade Creightney, Jemmy Jibowu, Gary Mangan, Daniel Matthews, Elen Rhys, Graham Roberts, Faye Siggers, Kirsty Spiers, Amy Stone, and Gary Waters from St. John the Baptist C. of E. School. They would also like to thank the Early Learning Centre, London, and Broadhurst, Clarkson and Fuller, London, for the loan of props.

Gareth Stevens Publishing would like to thank noted science author Greg Walz-Chojnacki for his assistance with the accuracy of the text. Mr. Walz-Chojnacki is the author of *Celestial Delights: The Best Astronomical Events Through 2001* and *Comet: The Story Behind Halley's Comet*.

**For a free color catalog describing Gareth Stevens' list of high-quality books and multimedia programs, call 1-800-542-2595 (USA) or 1-800-461-9120 (Canada). Gareth Stevens Publishing's Fax: (414) 225-0377. See our catalog, too, on the World Wide Web: http://gsinc.com**

Library of Congress Cataloging-in-Publication Data

Kerrod, Robin.
Astronomy / by Robin Kerrod.
p. cm. — (Young scientist concepts and projects)
Includes bibliographical references and index.
Summary: Provides an introduction to astronomy, including information about the solar system, stars and constellations, and projects such as making a sundial.
ISBN 0-8368-2083-5 (lib. bdg.)
1. Astronomy—Juvenile literature.   2. Astronomy—Experiments—Juvenile literature.   3. Astronomy—Observers' manuals—Juvenile literature.   [1. Astronomy.   2. Astronomy projects.   3. Science projects.]   I. Title.   II. Series.
QB46.A415   1998
520—dc21               97-41628

This North American edition first published in 1998 by
**Gareth Stevens Publishing**
1555 North RiverCenter Drive, Suite 201
Milwaukee, WI  53212  USA

Original edition © 1996 by Anness Publishing Limited. First published in 1996 by Lorenz Books, an imprint of Anness Publishing Inc., New York, New York. This U.S. edition © 1998 by Gareth Stevens, Inc. Additional end matter © 1998 by Gareth Stevens, Inc.

Senior Editor: Caroline Beattie
Photographer: John Freeman
Stylists: Thomasina Smith and Isolde Sommerfeldt
Designer: Caroline Reeves
Picture Researcher: Liz Eddison
Illustrator: Alisa Tingley
Gareth Stevens series editor: Dorothy L. Gibbs
Editorial assistant: Diane Laska

Printed in the United States of America

1 2 3 4 5 6 7 8 9 02 01 00 99 98

YOUNG SCIENTIST CONCEPTS & PROJECTS

# ASTRONOMY

## CONTENTS

# THE MAGNIFICENT HEAVENS

THE night sky is one of the great delights of nature. There is always something fascinating to see there. The stars wheel overhead as the night goes by, bright planets stand out like beacons, meteors burn up and leave fiery trails, the Moon waxes and wanes, comets suddenly appear and, just as suddenly, disappear. It is no wonder that people through the ages have studied the starry skies – the heavens – closely. Studying the heavens is a science called astronomy. Using their eyes, telescopes, satellites, and other equipment, astronomers have built a clear picture of what our universe is like.

*Part of a star map dating from the early 1700s, showing fanciful figures for the star patterns (constellations).*

**Star positions**
This is an ancient astronomical instrument called an astrolabe. Early astronomers used astrolabes to observe the positions of heavenly bodies.

### Ancient monuments
About 4,000 years ago, ancient Egyptians built their pyramids (*above*) to line up with certain stars. At about the same time, the ancient Britons started to build Stonehenge (*below*), near Salisbury, as a kind of astronomical observatory.

### Space travel
Astronomers now use space satellites to study the heavenly bodies. The satellites carry telescopes and other instruments into space. There, the heavens can be viewed more closely.

### Modern observatories
Astronomers work at observatories, such as Palomar in California (*right*). The dome houses a large telescope, which gathers the faint light stars give out.

# GETTING STARTED

STARGAZING is a great hobby, and you do not need a lot of expensive equipment for it. Just go outside on a clear, dark night and look up at the sky. The starry heavens look great no matter where you happen to live in the world. However, you will enjoy an evening's stargazing more if you spend a little time preparing for it. The main thing you need to do is make sure you are warm, because you will be standing or sitting outside for a long time. The best stargazing nights are usually the coldest, because clear skies have no clouds, which often act as a blanket to keep the Earth warm. So you will need warm clothes and hot drinks.

*The heavens look great just using your eyes. But when you look at them through binoculars, they look magnificent.*

## M A T E R I A L S

*You will need: binoculars, bag, gloves, scarf, warm headgear, thermos with hot drink, snack.*

### Get comfortable
You need to be as comfortable as possible when you go stargazing. In the yard, a lawn chair is ideal. If you venture farther away, a camping stool is easier to carry. And remember your star map!

M A T E R I A L S

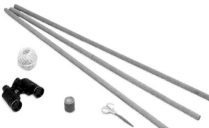

*You will need: 3 broom handles, strong tape, twine, scissors, binoculars.*

### Mount your binoculars

You will enjoy stargazing more when you use binoculars. Good binoculars, however, are quite heavy. Holding them up to your eyes for more than a few minutes is tiring. So, it is a good idea to make a simple tripod on which to mount them.

### Support your binoculars

To make the tripod, tape together the top ends of three broom handles. Spread the bottom ends out in a triangular shape until the top is at the right height for your eyes. Secure the handles with twine to keep them from spreading farther apart. When you have made your tripod, mount your binoculars on top. Tie them in position with twine. Make sure that the focusing ring on top of the binoculars is free to move.

*A planisphere is a useful aid to stargazing. It shows you which stars to look for in the sky at any time of the year.*

# PATTERNS IN THE SKY

THE night sky is full of stars. If you could count them, you would find that you can see several thousand at a time with the naked eye. Not all stars are the same. Some are much brighter than others. The bright stars form patterns in the sky. If you are a keen stargazer, you quickly can learn to recognize the star patterns. They will help you find your way through the night sky. We call these star patterns the constellations. They change little year after year. Over 2,000 years ago, the astronomers of Ancient Greece saw much the same constellations as we do. They gave the constellations the names we use today. They named them after the people, animals, and objects they thought the patterns looked like. They also made up stories about how these figures got into the heavens.

**Taurus, the Bull**

*Leo, the Lion*
*The pattern of stars in the constellation Leo look like the front part of a crouching lion.*

*Ancient astronomers pictured Orion as a mighty hunter (below).*

**Find Orion**
Orion is one of the easiest constellations to recognize in the night sky *(left)*. It can be seen well in both the Northern and the Southern hemispheres. The diagram *(right)* shows the pattern made by Orion's brightest stars.

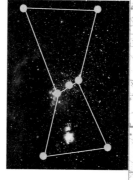

ORION

*Aquarius,
the Water-bearer*

*Cancer, the Crab*

*Stars in the night sky*

**Zodiac**
During the
year, the Sun
passes through
12 constellations.
They are known
as the constellations
of the zodiac. They
are important
in astrology.

*Celestial equator*

*Earth's Equator*

*Capricorn,
the Sea Goat*

**Celestial sphere**
The constellations move overhead as the night
goes by. The stars seem to be stuck on the inside
of a dark ball that is spinning around the Earth.
Ancient astronomers called this ball the celestial sphere.
But, in fact, it does not exist. The night sky appears
to spin around because the Earth itself is spinning.

*The celestial
sphere seems to spin
around Earth from east to
west. But, in fact, it is the Earth
that is spinning from west to east.*

# PHOTOGRAPHING THE STARS

*You will need: camera, rolls of ordinary film, shutter-release cable, tripod.*

YOU can take photographs of the night sky with simple equipment and ordinary film. To photograph the stars, you need a camera with a time-exposure (B setting). Because the stars do not give out much light, you have to keep the camera shutter open for quite a long time before the stars show up on film. You also need to mount the camera on a tripod to keep it steady while you have the shutter open. The tripod stops the camera from wobbling and blurring your picture. Use a shutter-release cable for the same reason.

*Stars make trails (above) in a picture taken with a camera pointing at the horizon.*

### Photograph the night sky

1 First, make sure your camera is loaded with film. Screw the shutter-release cable into the camera shutter. Then screw the camera in place on top of the tripod.

2 Using the "tilt" handle on the tripod, line up the camera with the horizon and tighten the clamp. Make sure that nothing blocks your view!

3 Press the shutter-release cable to open the shutter. Tighten the release in the open position. Leave it open for some time, from seconds to an hour. Then, close the shutter.

**4** Use the tilt handle again to point the camera upward at an angle of about 45 degrees. Tighten the clamp and advance the film.

**5** Repeat step 3. Again, try leaving the shutter open for different lengths of time, from several seconds to an hour or so.

*Stars go around in circles* (above) *in a picture taken with a camera pointing upward into the sky.*

**Not really a star**
The morning star and evening star are really a planet – Venus. It earned these names because, at times, Venus shines brightly at dawn and, at other times, at twilight.

# NORTHERN CONSTELLATIONS

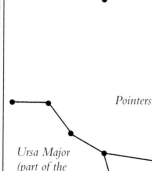

Northern celestial hemisphere

Earth

On these pages, we talk about constellations of the northern celestial hemisphere.

**B**ECAUSE the Earth is round, you can see only part of the celestial sphere at any time. People in Canada, for example, will not be able to see the constellations that people in New Zealand can see, because Canada is in the far Northern Hemisphere of the world and New Zealand is in the far Southern Hemisphere. Just as we divide the world into two halves, north and south, so we divide the celestial sphere into two hemispheres. The star map *(next page)* shows the constellations visible in the northern celestial hemisphere. They are often called northern constellations.

Ursa Minor
(Little Dipper or Little Bear)

North Star

Pointers

Ursa Major
(part of the Big Dipper or Great Bear)

*The Great Bear, or Big Dipper,* (above, right) *and the Northern Crown* (right), *as they appear on an old star map.*

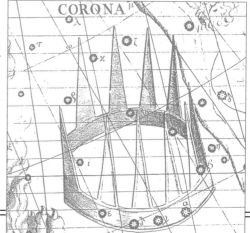

**Finding stars**
The stars in some constellations act as signposts to help us find the stars in other constellations. Two stars in Ursa Major help us find the North Star.

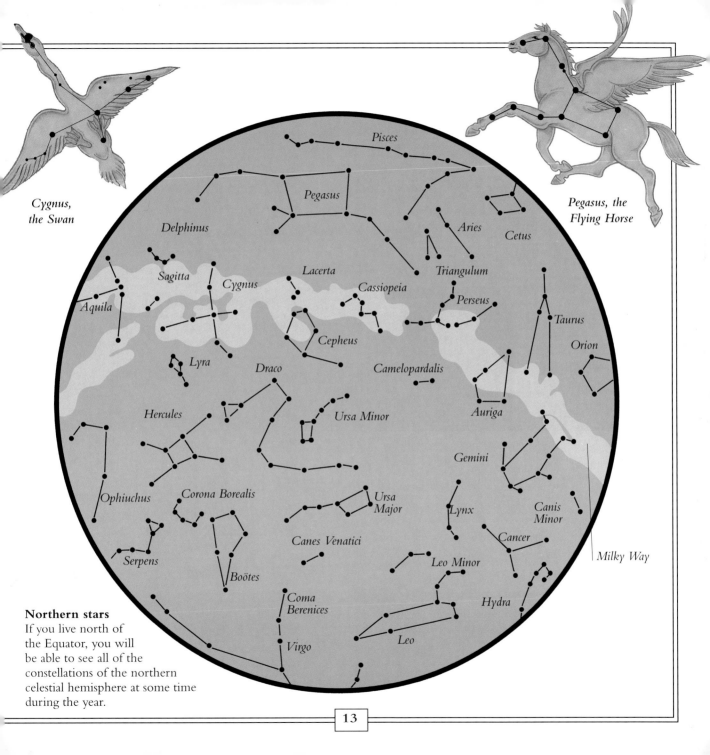

Cygnus,
the Swan

Pegasus, the
Flying Horse

Pisces

Pegasus

Delphinus

Aries

Cetus

Sagitta

Lacerta

Triangulum

Cygnus

Cassiopeia

Perseus

Aquila

Taurus

Cepheus

Orion

Lyra

Draco

Camelopardalis

Hercules

Ursa Minor

Auriga

Gemini

Ophiuchus

Corona Borealis

Ursa
Major

Lynx

Canis
Minor

Cancer

Serpens

Canes Venatici

Milky Way

Boötes

Leo Minor

Coma
Berenices

Hydra

**Northern stars**
If you live north of
the Equator, you will
be able to see all of the
constellations of the northern
celestial hemisphere at some time
during the year.

Virgo

Leo

# SOUTHERN CONSTELLATIONS

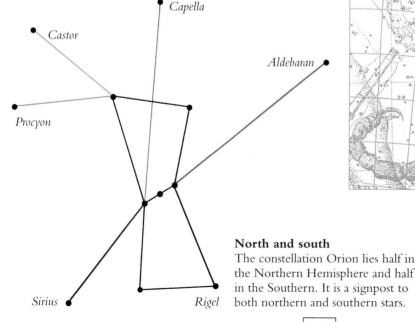

Earth

Southern celestial hemisphere

THIS star map *(next page)* shows constellations of the southern celestial hemisphere. They include such splendid constellations as Scorpius, the Scorpion, and Centaurus, the Centaur. Southern skies are, in general, more brilliant than northern ones and have the three brightest stars in the heavens – Sirius, Canopus, and Alpha Centauri. The northern and southern parts of the celestial sphere meet at what is called the celestial equator. Constellations around the celestial equator can be seen by both northern and southern astronomers at certain times of the year.

*On these pages, we talk about constellations of the southern celestial hemisphere.*

Capella

Castor

Aldebaran

Procyon

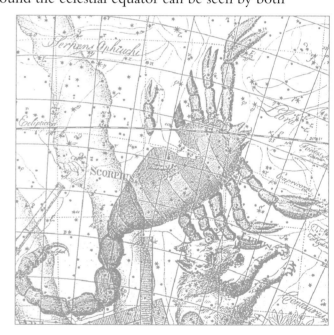

The constellation Scorpius, the Scorpion, pictured on an ancient star map.

Sirius

Rigel

**North and south**
The constellation Orion lies half in the Northern Hemisphere and half in the Southern. It is a signpost to both northern and southern stars.

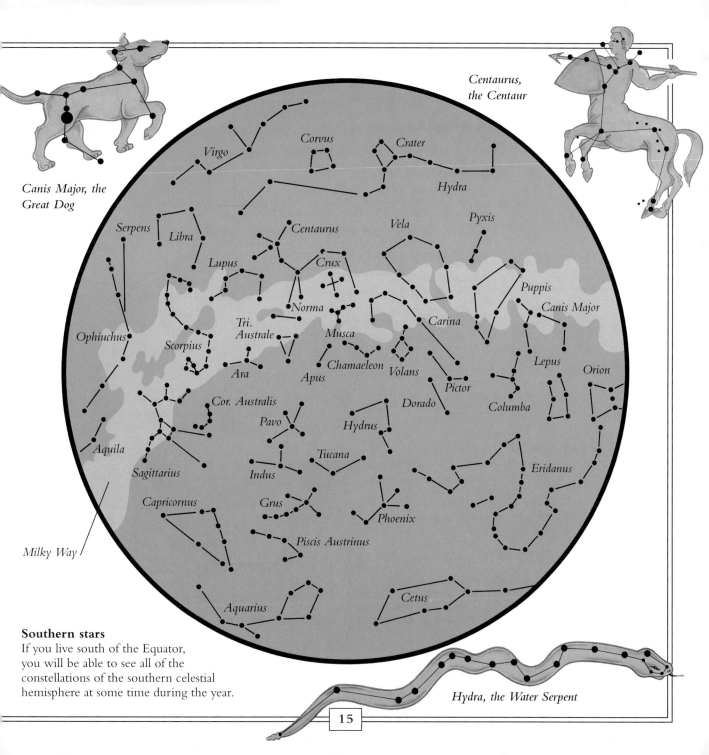

Canis Major, the
Great Dog

Centaurus,
the Centaur

Virgo

Corvus

Crater

Hydra

Serpens

Libra

Centaurus

Vela

Pyxis

Lupus

Crux

Ophiuchus

Norma

Scorpius

Tri.
Australe

Musca

Carina

Canis Major

Puppis

Ara

Apus

Chamaeleon

Volans

Lepus

Orion

Aquila

Cor. Australis

Pavo

Hydrus

Pictor

Dorado

Columba

Sagittarius

Indus

Tucana

Eridanus

Capricornus

Grus

Phoenix

Milky Way

Piscis Austrinus

Aquarius

Cetus

**Southern stars**
If you live south of the Equator,
you will be able to see all of the
constellations of the southern celestial
hemisphere at some time during the year.

Hydra, the Water Serpent

# MAKE A NIGHT SKY

Y OU can become more familiar with the night sky by drawing pictures of it and putting them on the walls – maybe even on the ceiling – of your room. But ask your parents first! Select the part of the night sky you want to show by looking at a star map or a planisphere. Then draw the star patterns (constellations) onto dark blue cardboard. You also can add some of the other things you might see in the heavens, such as comets and meteors. Use fluorescent materials, if possible, so you can see the heavenly bodies shine in your night sky.

## MATERIALS

*You will need: dark blue cardboard, fluorescent stick-on stars and dots, fluorescent paints, paintbrushes.*

*Use a planisphere to choose the star patterns you want to copy.*

### Make a star map

**1** Copy the star patterns from a star map onto the dark blue cardboard. Link the stars with your own shapes if you want to.

**2** Arrange stick-on stars and dots in the star patterns. Use different colored dots where you want to. Real stars have different colors.

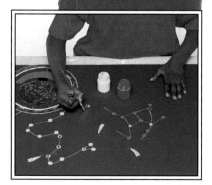

**3** When you have finished your star patterns, add objects, such as comets. Use stars for their heads and paint for their tails.

## Stars in 3D

From the Earth, it looks as if the stars are stuck on the inside of a huge overturned bowl. They all seem to be the same distance away, and they do not seem to move. In fact, the stars are all at different distances away from us, and they do move. We cannot see them move because they are too far away. This mobile will give you an idea of how the stars are arranged in space.

### Make a mobile

MATERIALS

You will need: wire, bowl, tape, thread, ping-pong balls, fluorescent paints, paintbrushes, glue.

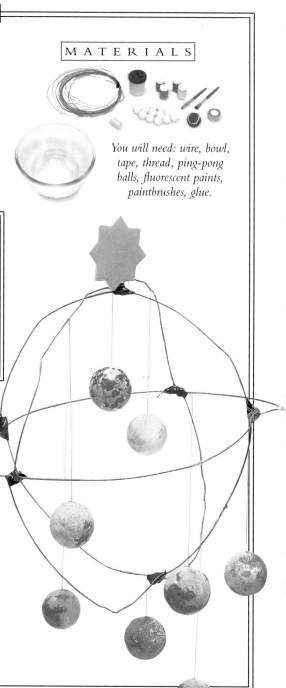

1 Make three circles with the wire. Wrap the wire around the bowl to get the right size and shape. Tie or tape the wire circles together to form a ball shape.

2 Paint the ping-pong balls with fluorescent paint – use lots of colors. Tie or glue a different length of thread to each ball.

3 Tie the painted ping-pong balls to the wire circles. Then hang your mobile from the ceiling. It shows how the stars are scattered around in space, all at different distances from the Earth. Spin it, and you will see the stars move.

# SEASONAL STARS

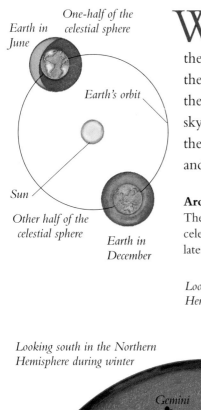

*Earth in June*

*One-half of the celestial sphere*

*Earth's orbit*

*Sun*

*Other half of the celestial sphere*

*Earth in December*

W E see different constellations in the night sky season by season, because, at different times of the year, we look at different parts of the celestial sphere. If you live in the Northern Hemisphere, you will see the greatest changes in the night sky when you look south. If you live in the Southern Hemisphere, you will see the greatest changes in the night sky when you look north. The star maps on these two pages show how the constellations change between summer and winter in the Northern and Southern hemispheres.

**Around the Sun**
The Earth circles around the Sun once a year. At any time, we can see only half of the celestial sphere. We cannot see the other half because the Sun blocks it out. Six months later, we can see the other half, while the Sun blocks out the first half.

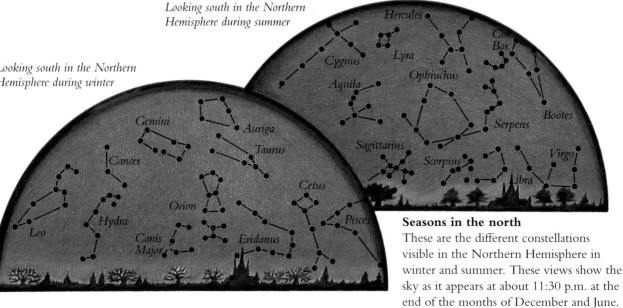

*Looking south in the Northern Hemisphere during summer*

*Looking south in the Northern Hemisphere during winter*

Hercules

Cor. Bor.

Cygnus

Lyra

Ophiuchus

Aquila

Boötes

Serpens

Sagittarius

Virgo

Scorpius

Libra

Gemini

Auriga

Cancer

Taurus

Cetus

Orion

Pisces

Leo

Hydra

Canis Major

Eridanus

**Seasons in the north**
These are the different constellations visible in the Northern Hemisphere in winter and summer. These views show the sky as it appears at about 11:30 p.m. at the end of the months of December and June.

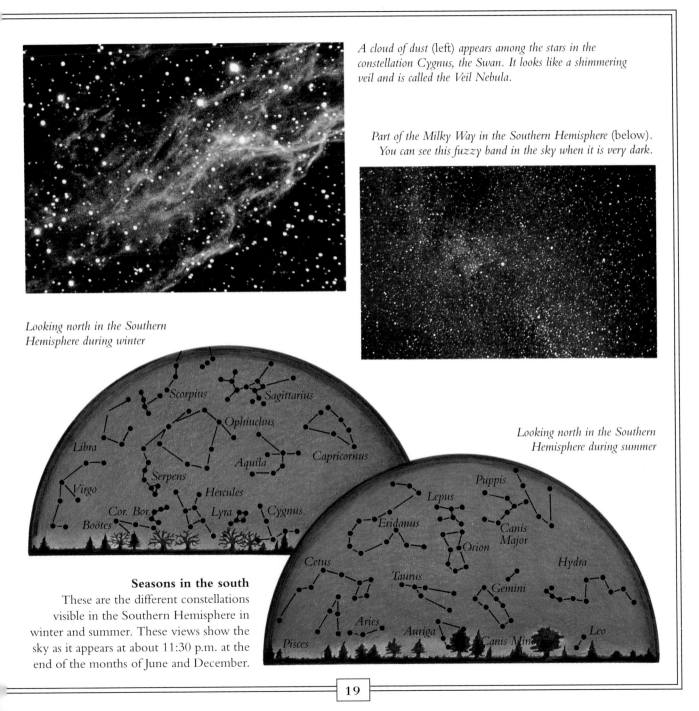

*A cloud of dust (left) appears among the stars in the constellation Cygnus, the Swan. It looks like a shimmering veil and is called the Veil Nebula.*

*Part of the Milky Way in the Southern Hemisphere (below). You can see this fuzzy band in the sky when it is very dark.*

*Looking north in the Southern Hemisphere during winter*

*Looking north in the Southern Hemisphere during summer*

### Seasons in the south

These are the different constellations visible in the Southern Hemisphere in winter and summer. These views show the sky as it appears at about 11:30 p.m. at the end of the months of June and December.

# USING A PLANISPHERE

A planisphere will help you find your way around the heavens. It consists of two disks held together in the center. The top disk has a window and a scale marked with times of the day and night. The bottom disk has a star map and a scale marked with days of the year. When you move the disks to line up the time and the day you want to stargaze, the stars to watch for appear in the window. Different stars can be seen from different parts of the world, or latitudes. So there are different planispheres for different latitudes.

You will need: planisphere,
watch or clock, compass.

*Three planispheres
for different latitudes*

### Finding stars

**1** Suppose you want to go stargazing on September 15. Get out your planisphere and check the time. Let us say it is 11 p.m.

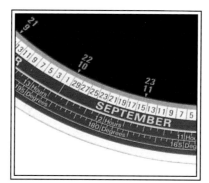

**2** Suppose you live in the Northern Hemisphere at about latitude 42° north. Turn the disks until 11 on the top disk lines up with September 15 on the bottom disk. The stars visible at this time will appear in the window.

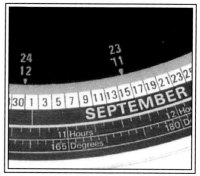

**3** Suppose you live in the Southern Hemisphere at about latitude 35° south. Turn the disks until 11 on the top disk lines up with September 15 on the bottom disk. The stars visible at this time will appear in the window.

### North or south?

If you live in the Northern Hemisphere, hold the planisphere above your head, face down, so that "midnight" on the top scale points north. The planisphere is now in the right position. If you live in the Southern Hemisphere, hold the planisphere so that "midnight" on the top scale points south. The planisphere is now in the right position.

*Window on the night sky from latitude 42° north at 11 p.m. on September 15.*

**4** Now, check a compass to determine which direction is north and which is south. This helps you position your planisphere properly, so that the window shows the sky the right way up.

*Window on the night sky from latitude 35° south at 11 p.m. on September 15.*

# WHAT STARS ARE LIKE

To our eyes, the stars are tiny pinpoints of light, but, in fact, they are very vast. They are bodies like our Sun, made up of hot, glowing gases. Like the Sun, they give off energy as light, heat, and other forms of radiation. The reason stars appear to be so tiny is because they are so far away. Even nearby stars are over 25 trillion miles (40 trillion kilometers) away. It takes a beam of light from these stars more than four years to reach us. So astronomers say that these stars lie over four light-years away. They use the "light-year" as a unit to measure distances to the stars.

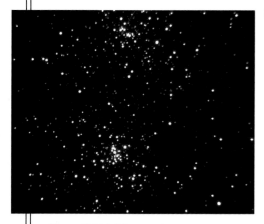

*Some of the bright stars in the constellation Perseus.*

**Space travel**
Imagine riding in a starship that could travel at the speed of light. This speed is 186,000 miles (299,274 km) per second. It would take you just eight and a half minutes to travel to the Sun. It would take you more than four years to reach even the next nearest star!

*Starship*

*Earth*

**Bright and dim**
In the night sky, some stars look brighter than others. But a star that looks bright may not really be brighter than a star that looks dim. The star that looks dim might be a truly bright star that is long, long way off. The star that looks bright might be a truly dim star that is quite close to Earth.

*The nearest star to the Sun is a small, faint red star called Proxima Centauri.*

*Nearest star*

## Star sizes

Stars come in all sizes. Our local star, the Sun, has a diameter of about 868,000 miles (1,400,000 km). It is more than 100 times bigger than the Earth's diameter. But, compared with many other stars, the Sun is tiny, as the picture *(below)* shows. Astronomers call the Sun a dwarf star. Stars called red giants are much bigger, and stars called supergiants are unbelievably big. Supergiants can measure hundreds of millions of miles (kilometers) across.

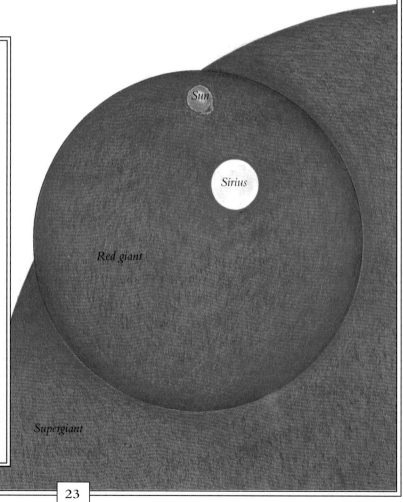

*Sun*

*Sirius*

*Red giant*

*Supergiant*

### BRIGHTEST STARS

| Star | Constellation | Magnitude★ |
|------|---------------|-----------|
| Sirius | Canis Major | -1.4 |
| Canopus | Carina | -0.7 |
| Alpha Centauri | Centaurus | -0.2 |
| Arcturus | Boötes | -0.1 |
| Vega | Lyra | 0.0 |
| Capella | Auriga | 0.1 |

★ The brightness of a star is measured on a scale of magnitude. The brightest stars we see are of magnitude 1 or below. The faintest ones are of magnitude 6.

### NEAREST STARS

| Star | Constellation | Distance★ (light-years) |
|------|---------------|-------------------------|
| Prox. Centauri | Centaurus | 4.3 |
| Alpha Centauri | Centaurus | 4.3 |
| Bernard's star | Ophiuchus | 5.8 |
| Wolf 359 | Leo | 7.6 |
| Lalande 21185 | Ursa Major | 8.1 |
| Sirius | Canis Major | 8.7 |

★ 1 light-year is the distance light travels in a year, nearly 6 trillion miles (9.6 trillion km).

# CLUSTERS AND CLOUDS

Many stars travel through space in groups. Some travel in groups of twos and threes, but others travel in groups of hundreds and even thousands. We call these large groups of stars clusters. In many groups, the stars are quite far apart. We call these groups open clusters. In other groups, the stars are packed closely together to form large globes. We call these groups globular clusters.

Clusters are found among the constellations, so are objects called nebulas. The word *nebula* means "cloud." Nebulas are large clouds of gas and dust. Bright nebulas are illuminated by nearby stars. Dark nebulas can be seen only when they block the light from stars behind them.

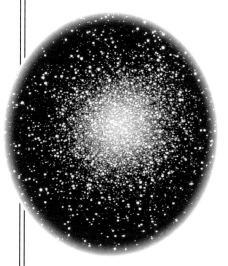

*This great mass of stars is a globular cluster. It contains hundreds of thousands of stars packed closely together.*

*The Ring Nebula looks like a smoke ring. It really is a bubble of gas puffed out by a star in the center.*

*This nebula is called the Tarantula, because it looks like the large, hairy spider of the same name. It is found in a galaxy called the Large Magellanic Cloud.*

**Bright nebula**
The Orion Nebula in the constellation Orion is one of the few we can see with the naked eye. But only photographs taken through telescopes show its true beauty.

The stars in this open cluster sparkle like jewels, and it is often called the Jewel Box. It can be seen only in the Southern Hemisphere because it is in the far southern constellation Crux, the Southern Cross.

Also in the constellation Orion is the Horsehead Nebula. It is a mass of dark gas in the shape of a horse's head.

# GALAXIES OF STARS

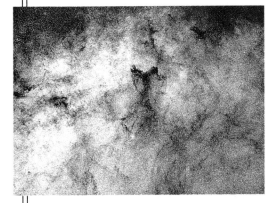

THE Sun and all the stars we see in the night sky belong to one great star system. The whole system is called a galaxy. Through very powerful telescopes, we can see many other galaxies like it. Between them, there is empty space. Our own galaxy is called the Milky Way. This is also the name of the band of faint light that arches across the heavens, which we can see on a very dark night. Through binoculars, we can see that this band is made up of millions of stars, seemingly packed closely together.

*A photograph of the Milky Way shows that it is made up of millions and millions of stars.*

## Milky Way

In our galaxy, most of the stars are grouped on curved or spiral arms coming out of the center. If you could view it from the side, it would look something like this *(above)*. When you look at the Milky Way in the night sky, you really are looking at a cross-section, or slice, through the disk of our galaxy.

## GALAXY TYPES

Our galaxy has a spiral shape. There are many other spiral galaxies like it in the heavens. Another kind of spiral galaxy is called a barred spiral. The arms come out of a bar through the bulge at the center.

A third common type is the elliptical galaxy, which may be round or oval in shape. It does not have any arms.

There are also irregular galaxies, which have no particular shape at all.

*Spiral*

*Barred spiral*

*Elliptical*

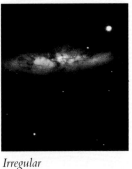

*Irregular*

## Spiral galaxy

Our galaxy, the Milky Way, is a spiral galaxy. At the center is a great bulge of stars, and there are more stars farther out. They form long, curving (or spiral) arms. The Sun is found on one of these arms, quite a long way from the center. The whole galaxy is rotating. If we could see it from a distance, it would look like a spinning pinwheel firework. Our galaxy is gigantic. It is made up of at least 100,000 million stars. It is so big that it would take a beam of light 100 million years to travel from one side to the other.

*This galaxy is found in the constellation Andromeda. It is a spiral galaxy like our own. Our galaxy would look like this from a great distance.*

# THE BOUNDLESS UNIVERSE

WE know that the universe is made up of planets, moons, stars, nebulas, and galaxies traveling through space. But most of the universe is just empty space. How big is the universe? No one really knows. Astronomers already have detected objects over 10,000 million light-years away.

*All galaxies are made up of millions of stars, which were born in the great clouds of gas and dust called nebulas. This is the Lagoon Nebula in the constellation Sagittarius.*

*Earth*

*Solar system*

*Stars*

*Milky Way Galaxy*

*Local Group*

**Solar system**
In our corner of the universe, the Earth is one of nine planets circling the Sun. The Sun is a star, like the thousands we see in the night sky. All these stars form part of the Milky Way Galaxy. It is one of a small cluster of galaxies called the Local Group. About 30 galaxies make up the Local Group. The largest ones are spirals like the Milky Way and the Andromeda Galaxy.

*The Andromeda Galaxy is one of the nearest galaxies to Earth. We can see it with the naked eye as a fuzzy patch in the constellation Andromeda. It is one of a small cluster of galaxies in the Local Group.*

*Expanding universe*

Big Bang

## The Big Bang

Many astronomers believe that the universe was born 15-20 billion years ago. It started, they say, with a gigantic explosion they call the Big Bang. After a while, galaxies, stars, planets, and moons formed. The Big Bang started the universe expanding. It is still expanding today.

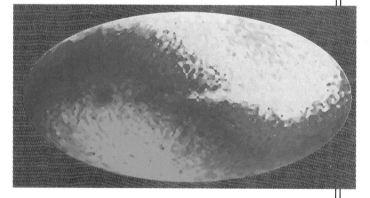

*In recent years, spacecraft like COBE have sent back information that suggests there was a Big Bang. This (right) is one of the radiation maps of the entire sky sent back by COBE.*

# EXPANDING THE UNIVERSE

W HEN astronomers study galaxies, they find all the galaxies are moving away from Earth, and away from one another, at very high speeds. The universe is expanding. Think of the universe as a balloon being blown up bigger and bigger. If we blow up the balloon too much, it might burst. Could the universe end up doing that?

*Have fun with balloons, and discover the secrets of the universe!*

### MATERIALS

*You will need: round balloons, stick-on spots, string, scissors.*

## Make a universe

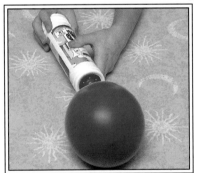

**1** Partly blow up a round balloon. Puff into it gradually yourself, or use an air pump, if you want to.

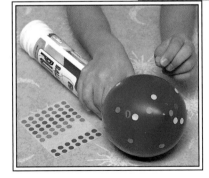

**2** Stick spots on the partly blown-up balloon. Place them equal distances apart. Think of the balloon as the universe – the spots are the galaxies.

**3** Blow up the balloon some more. Watch it get bigger and the spots move farther apart – the universe is expanding!

## Are there other universes?

We think we know what our universe is like. But is it the only universe? Scientists used to think our galaxy was the only galaxy. Now we know of millions like it. So some astronomers are wondering whether our universe is just one of many in a kind of super, multiple universe. Build a super, multiple universe yourself. Make a number of balloon universes like the one shown on these two pages. Tie them together with string. Think of the strings as pathways between the universes. Maybe, one day, astronomers will find pathways like them.

**4** When the balloon is really big, pinch the neck to keep the air in the balloon.

**5** Now let go of the neck so that the air rushes out. The balloon gets smaller and smaller, and the spots get closer together.

**6** The balloon universe is shrinking, and its galaxies are coming closer together. Some astronomers think this might happen to the real universe in the distant future.

# OUR LOCAL STAR

*The Sun glows fiery red just before it sets in the western sky. It does not look very big from the Earth. But it is huge. It could swallow more than a million Earths!*

**Seething surface**
The surface of the Sun is a seething mass of boiling gases. In places, great fiery fountains, called prominences, leap thousands of miles (km) above the surface (*below*). Smaller flares (*right*) spring up all over it.

THE most important body in our corner of the universe is the Sun, our local star. It appears to be much bigger and brighter than the other stars because it is much closer. The Sun is about 93 million miles (150 million km) away from the Earth, which is only a tiny fraction of the distance to the next nearest star. The Sun is much bigger than the Earth, with a diameter of 868,000 miles (1,400,000 km). Astronomers believe that the Sun has been shining for more than 5 billion years and will continue to shine 5 billion years more.

Prominence

Sunspot

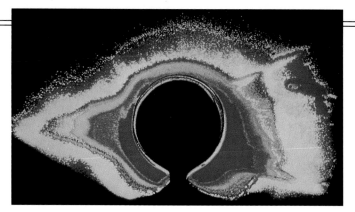

### The Sun's crown
Astronauts in the *Skylab* space station carried out detailed studies of the Sun in 1973. They took many dramatic pictures. This one shows the corona (the outer atmosphere of the Sun).

*If you have a telescope, you can view sunspots projected onto a sheet of paper. You need a piece of cardboard to shade the sheet of paper.*

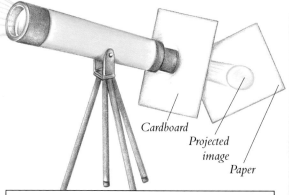

Cardboard

Projected image

Paper

### Space station
NASA's *Skylab* space station in orbit in 1973. Three teams of astronauts spent 28, 59, and 84 days, in turn, carrying out observations and experiments.

---

### WARNING!
- **Never look at the Sun directly with your eyes or through binoculars or a telescope.**
- **The Sun is so bright that its light can blind you.**
- **The only safe way to view the Sun is by projection, like in the diagram** *above.*

### Lights in space
Astronauts also have taken pictures of the aurora. This glow in the sky takes place at the North and South poles when particles from the Sun collide with air particles in the Earth's atmosphere.

# SUN AND EARTH

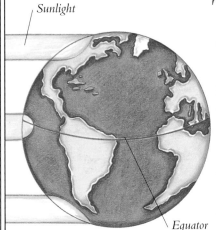

Sunlight

Equator

*The heat in a sunbeam spreads over a greater area the farther away from the Equator.*

THE Sun keeps the Earth alive. Without the Sun's heat and light, the Earth would be a cold and lifeless lump of rock. It would be lifeless because living things need a reasonable temperature in which to live. Without sunlight, plants could not grow, and there would be no vegetation. Because the Earth is round, the Sun heats some parts of the Earth more than others. This gives rise to the different climates found on Earth. The hottest climates are around the Equator, and the coldest ones are at the North and South poles.

**Rainbow colors**
Sunlight is not golden, as you might think. It is made of the light of seven main colors. You see these colors in the rainbow. Raindrops split light into a rainbow, which has violet on the inside, then indigo, blue, green, yellow, orange, and, finally, red on the outside.

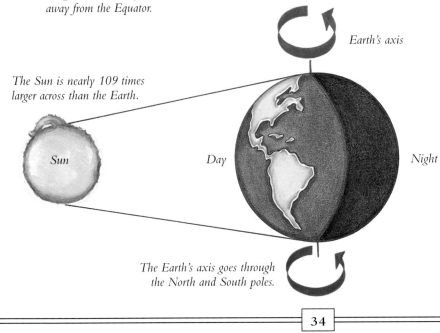

*The Sun is nearly 109 times larger across than the Earth.*

Sun

Day

Earth's axis

Night

*The Earth's axis goes through the North and South poles.*

**Night and day**
The Sun's light illuminates half of the Earth at any time. For this half, it is day. The side of the Earth away from the Sun is in darkness. For that side, it is night. But, because the Earth is spinning around on its axis, both sides have day and night in turn.

## Seasons

The Earth's axis is tilted in space, so each half of the Earth tilts more toward the Sun at some times of the year than at others. This makes each half hotter at some times than at others. Such changes in temperature mark what are called the seasons. The hottest time of the year is the season of summer. The coldest is winter. Midway between winter and summer is spring. Midway between summer and winter is autumn.

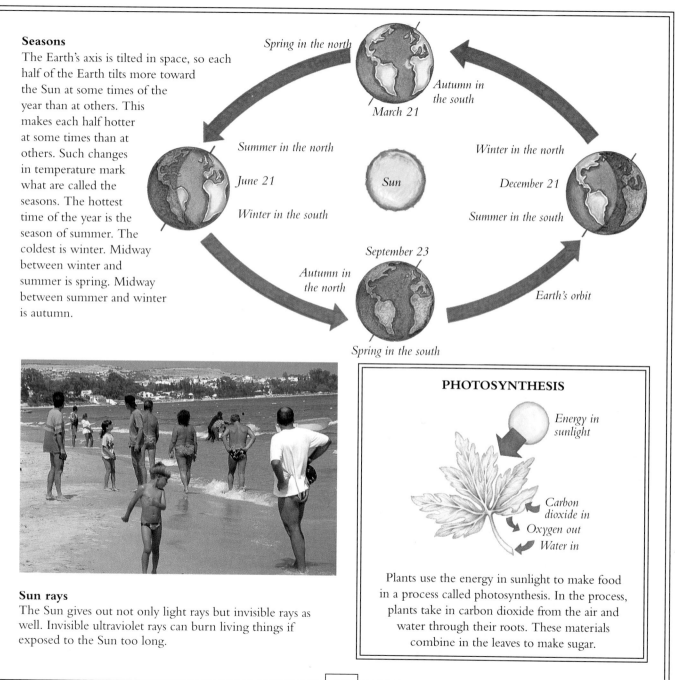

*Spring in the north*

*Autumn in the south*

*March 21*

*Summer in the north*

*June 21*

*Winter in the south*

*Sun*

*Winter in the north*

*December 21*

*Summer in the south*

*September 23*

*Autumn in the north*

*Spring in the south*

*Earth's orbit*

## Sun rays

The Sun gives out not only light rays but invisible rays as well. Invisible ultraviolet rays can burn living things if exposed to the Sun too long.

## PHOTOSYNTHESIS

*Energy in sunlight*

*Carbon dioxide in*

*Oxygen out*

*Water in*

Plants use the energy in sunlight to make food in a process called photosynthesis. In the process, plants take in carbon dioxide from the air and water through their roots. These materials combine in the leaves to make sugar.

# MAKING SUNDIALS

Thousands of years ago, people used shadows to tell the time of day. They built simple shadow clocks. There was an upright piece called a gnomon, which cast shadows on a scale marking the time of day. Later, more accurate sundials were made, which had sloping gnomons. There are many old sundials of this kind still in existence. With the following project, you can make both a simple sundial and one you can carry around with you!

M A T E R I A L S

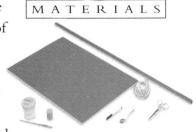

*You will need: wooden pole, paint, paintbrush, hammer, string, small piece of wood for a stake, 12 pieces of colored cardboard, marker pens.*

## Make a garden sundial

**1** Decorate the wooden pole, and pound it firmly into the ground. Tie one end of the string to the top of the pole. Then stake the other end into the ground, a pole's length away, on the south side of the pole.

**2** The string becomes your gnomon. Every hour, place cardboard with the time marked on it where the shadow of the gnomon falls. Here, the children are putting the 4 p.m. time card in place.

**3** After you have done this all through one day, your sundial will be ready for use. On sunny days, you will be able to tell the time by looking at the shadows rather than at your watch.

## Make a portable sundial

*You will need: a piece of colored cardboard, a compass, scissors, colored pencils and paints, paintbrush, ruler, glue, flowerpot, wooden dowel, magnetic compass.*

### Time for tea
This sundial is on the grounds of Herstmonceux Castle in southern England, the former site of the Royal Greenwich Observatory. The time is 16:00 hours, in other words, 4 p.m.

Use a compass to draw a circle on the cardboard. Cut around it to make a disk. On the disk, draw 12 evenly spaced marks for the hours of the day. Glue the disk on the overturned flowerpot. Push the dowel through the middle of the disk. (You might want to cut out the center of the cardboard first.) Now, place the pot in the sunlight. Look at a compass, and make a mark on the pot in the direction of north. Every hour during the day, mark where the shadow of the dowel falls on the edge of the disk. Your portable sundial is now ready for use. Every time you use it, make sure that the north mark on the pot points north, otherwise, your sundial will be off.

# THE MOON

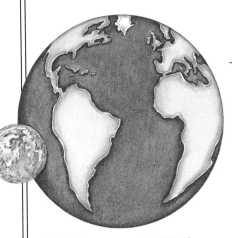

The Moon measures 2,155 miles (3,467 km) across, only about a quarter of the size of the Earth. Because it is so small, the Moon's gravity has a fairly weak pull.

WE know more about the Moon than about any other heavenly body because astronauts have landed on it and explored the surface. The Moon is our closest neighbor in space. It is Earth's only satellite. It circles the Earth at a distance of about 238,000 miles (383,000 km) and makes the journey about once a month. The Moon does not give out any light of its own. It is visible to us because it reflects light from the Sun. The sunlight illuminates different parts of the Moon as the month goes by, making the Moon seem to change shape. The Moon spins slowly as it circles the Earth, so the same side always faces the Earth. The picture on the next page shows what this near-side looks like. We see the moon fully illuminated only once a month.

Astronaut Neil Armstrong planted the first footprint on the Moon on July 20, 1969.

**Phases of the Moon**

The shape of the Moon appears to change during the month. We call these changes in shape the Moon's phases. It takes the Moon 29½ days to change from a slim crescent to a full circle and back again.

## TIDES

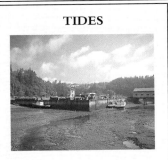

The Moon's pull causes the tides on Earth. When the Moon is overhead at the seaside, it pulls the water toward it, causing a high tide. Low tides occur when the Moon is elsewhere and pulls the water back *(above)*.

This Moon mountain, called Hadley Delta Mountain, rises to a height of more than 13,000 feet (4,000 meters). Mountains on the Moon rise to more than 19,000 feet (5,800 m).

## Full Moon

When the Moon is fully illuminated, we call it the full Moon. The darker regions on the surface are great dusty plains called seas, or maria. The lighter regions are highlands, pitted with craters sometimes hundreds of miles (km) across.

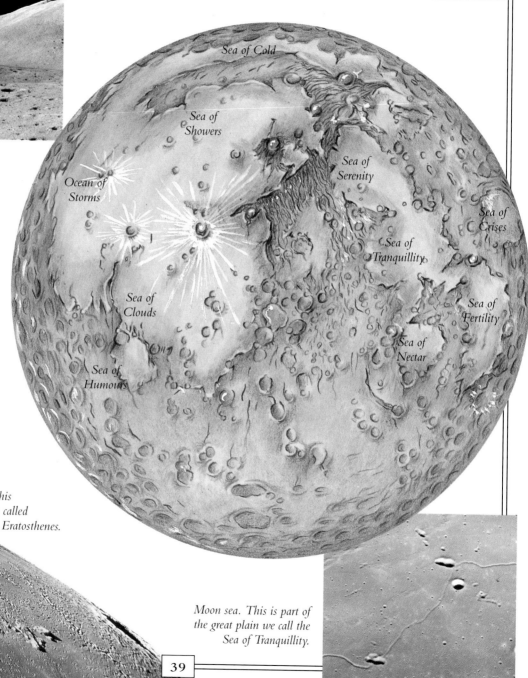

Sea of Cold

Sea of Showers

Sea of Serenity

Ocean of Storms

Sea of Crises

Sea of Tranquillity

Sea of Fertility

Sea of Clouds

Sea of Nectar

Sea of Humours

Moon crater. This crater is called Eratosthenes.

Moon sea. This is part of the great plain we call the Sea of Tranquillity.

# MOON MOVEMENTS

THE Moon travels around the Earth once a month and appears to change shape as it does so. You do not have to wait a month to see these changes in shape, or phases. You can carry out this project and watch the Moon go through its phases in a few minutes!

*Astronauts took this picture of the Moon when they flew around it in 1970.*

### MATERIALS

*You will need: soccer or beach ball, glue and brush, aluminum foil, flashlight.*

### Make your own Moon

**1** Brush glue all over the ball. Rest it on a flowerpot, or something similar, to keep it still.

**2** Wrap the ball with aluminum foil, making sure the foil is as smooth as possible. You now have your Moon!

**3** Place your Moon on a table. Wedge something underneath to stop it from rolling off.

*Crescent Moon*

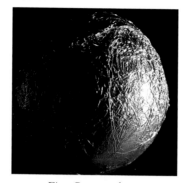

*First Quarter phase*

*Full Moon*

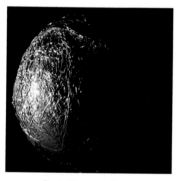

*Last Quarter phase*

*Crescent Moon*

### Going through the phases

When you stand opposite your friend, the side of your Moon facing you will be in darkness. This is what happens once a month in the night sky when the opposite side of the Moon is illuminated by the Sun. We cannot see the Moon, so we call it a new Moon. As you move around the table, you will see more and more of your Moon illuminated by the flashlight. All of it will be illuminated when you look from behind your friend. When this happens in the night sky, we call it a full Moon. As you continue moving around, after your "full Moon," you gradually will see less and less of it. Your Moon will disappear when you are opposite your friend again. It will be another new Moon.

**4** Ask a friend to shine a flashlight with a strong beam on your Moon. Stand opposite and look at your Moon with the lights out.

**5** With your friend standing still, walk around the table, still looking at your Moon, which is illuminated on one side by the flashlight.

# SHADOWS IN SPACE

THE Moon circles the Earth as the Earth circles the Sun. Once or twice a year, the Moon comes between the Sun and the Earth. It may completely or partially block the light from the Sun, leaving the Earth in shadow. We call this an eclipse of the Sun, or a solar eclipse. Also, at times, the Earth comes between the Sun and the Moon. It blots out the light from the Sun and leaves the Moon in shadow. We call this an eclipse of the Moon, or a lunar eclipse.

*Orbit of the Moon around the Earth*

*Sun*

*Moon*  *Umbra*

*Earth*

*Total eclipse of the Sun*

**Solar eclipse**
Eclipses of the Sun occur when the Moon casts a shadow on the Earth. A complete shadow, called an umbra, can be seen only over a small area. There, a total eclipse takes place. A part shadow, called a penumbra, can be seen over a much bigger area. There, a partial eclipse takes place.

**Lunar eclipse**
Eclipses of the Moon occur when the Moon passes into the shadow cast by the Earth. The Moon can stay in eclipse for a number of hours, because the Earth casts a big shadow in space. An eclipse of the Sun lasts only a few minutes at most, because the Moon casts such a small shadow.

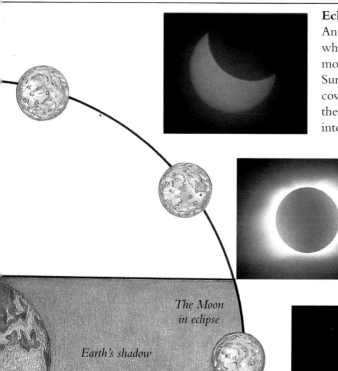

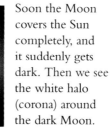

### Eclipse of the Sun
An eclipse of the Sun starts when the Moon begins to move across the face of the Sun. Gradually, the Moon covers more and more of the Sun, and daylight turns into twilight.

Soon the Moon covers the Sun completely, and it suddenly gets dark. Then we see the white halo (corona) around the dark Moon.

*An eclipse of the Moon begins when the Moon enters the Earth's shadow in space. During the eclipse, the Moon takes on a pinkish tinge (above).*

The Moon in eclipse

Earth's shadow

Next, the Sun begins to peep over the edge of the Moon. It looks like a sparkling diamond in a ring. That is why this stage of the eclipse is called the diamond ring.

Seconds later, the Moon moves on and uncovers more of the Sun. Daylight returns once more.

*The sky does not get completely dark during a solar eclipse. There is light in the distance around the horizon.*

43

# THE SUN'S FAMILY

THE Earth and the Sun travel through space together. The Earth is one of a family of bodies that circles the Sun in space. These bodies are called planets. Many of the planets have smaller bodies, called moons, circling them. All these bodies form part of the Sun's family, which is called the solar system. In addition to the planets, other bodies circle the Sun. Some are swarms of small bodies, called asteroids, and others are icy lumps, called comets. The whole solar system of planets, moons, asteroids, and comets is held together by the Sun's enormous pull (gravity).

*Saturn*

*Jupiter*

*Mercury*

*Venus*

*Earth*

*Mars*

*Sun*

**The planets**
The nine planets lie at different distances from the Sun. Nearest to the Sun is Mercury; farthest away is Pluto. The planets vary widely in size. The four planets closest to the Sun are much smaller than the next four, which are called the giant planets.

**The Sun**
The Sun lies at the heart of the solar system. It is not the same kind of body as the planets. It is a star, a great ball of glowing gases that gives out enormous energy as heat and light.

This diagram shows roughly to scale how far apart the planets are. The sizes of the planets are not drawn to scale.

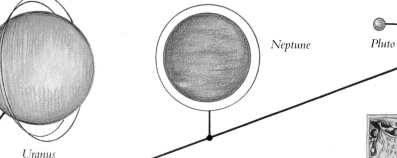

*Uranus*

*Neptune*

*Pluto*

## Tiny Pluto

Pluto is the most distant and, by far, the smallest planet. Even smaller bodies are found still farther away.

## Huge planets

The giant planets are truly gigantic and are quite unlike the Earth. They are made up mainly of gases, while the Earth is made up mainly of rock.

### FACT BOX

• The Sun is the only body in the solar system that gives out light. The other bodies shine because they reflect the Sun's light.

• Jupiter weighs more than all the other planets put together.

• Saturn is so light that, if you could put it in water, it would float.

• Mercury takes only 88 days to circle the Sun. Pluto takes nearly 250 years.

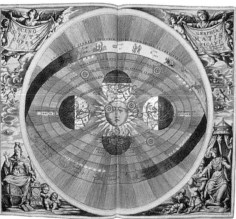

*It was not until the 1500s that astronomers, such as Copernicus, began to realize that the Earth and the other planets circle the Sun.*

*Ancient astronomers thought the Earth was the center of the universe. It seemed to them that the Sun, the Moon, the planets, and the stars circled the Earth.*

# SCALING THE SOLAR SYSTEM

*At the center of the solar system, the Sun sends rays of heat and light toward the planets.*

*Mercury, Venus, Earth, and Mars lie quite close to the Sun. Mercury and Venus are so close that they are baking hot. Earth is not too hot and not too cold. Living things like it here! They would not like Mars — it is too cold.*

THE planets are spread out over vast distances in space. It is difficult on two pages of a book to give a true impression of the scale of the solar system, but this project should help. The idea is for you and your friends to represent the planets and sit in a line at different distances from a friend who represents the Sun. The people playing Mercury, Venus, Earth, and Mars sit close together and close to the Sun. Those playing the other planets sit much farther apart. Use your imagination and cutting, painting, and pasting skills to make a hat showing which planet you are. This is what would happen if we used the same scale for the distances for Jupiter and the other planets as we do on this page for all the planets from Mercury to Mars. Jupiter would appear in the middle of page 48, Saturn on page 50, Uranus on page 54, Neptune on page 59, and we could not get Pluto in the book at all!

*You will need: colored paper, marker pens, colored pencils, scissors, ruler, colored tape, and stick-on dots and stars.*

## Four giants

The four planets close to the Sun are tiny compared with the next four planets. Jupiter, Saturn, Uranus, and Neptune are much bigger. They are also much farther apart from one another.

*Jupiter is the biggest planet of them all. If it had been much bigger when it formed, it might have become a star, not a planet.*

*Some people think Saturn is the most beautiful planet because of the shining rings surrounding it.*

*Uranus and its twin, Neptune, have rings around them, but we cannot see them from Earth. Here, Neptune is shown walking away because it is a lot farther away.*

*Pluto is the tiniest planet by far – it is smaller than Earth's Moon – and it lies a very long distance away. Here, Pluto has so far to go that it has to go on a skateboard!*

*Mercury*

*Venus*

*Earth*

*Mars*

*Jupiter*

*Saturn*

*Uranus*

*Neptune*

*Pluto*

# MERCURY, VENUS, AND EARTH

ERCURY, Venus, and Earth are the three planets closest to the Sun. Mercury and Venus are made of rock like the Earth and have a similar structure, but they are unlike the Earth in other ways. Mercury has a very hot, sun-baked surface and has no air, or atmosphere, around it. Venus is nearly the same size as the Earth and has an atmosphere, but its atmosphere is made of carbon dioxide and is very thick. The pressure would crush human beings. The atmosphere acts like a greenhouse, causing the planet's temperature to heat up like an oven.

*Mercury*

*Earth*

**Mercury**
Mercury looks much like the Moon because it is covered with many thousands of craters. The space probe *Mariner 10* sent back this picture (*above*) when it visited the planet in 1974.

**Small planet**
Compared with the Earth, Mercury is tiny. It is the second smallest planet, after Pluto. But, while Pluto is very cold, Mercury is very hot. In places, temperatures can rise to more than 842° Fahrenheit (450° Celsius).

*This picture* (right) *from Mariner 10 shows a close-up of Mercury's cratered surface. The craters measure up to 30 miles (48 km) across.*

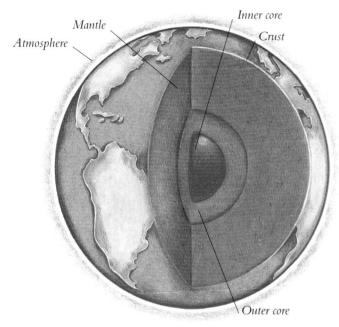

Atmosphere · Mantle · Inner core · Crust · Outer core

### Earth from space

Earth looks beautiful from space. This picture was taken by the Apollo astronauts. It shows most of Africa, Arabia, and Asia. Europe is mostly under clouds.

### Venus from space

We cannot see the surface of Venus from the Earth because thick clouds fill the atmosphere. The space probe *Mariner 10* took this photograph of Venus in 1974, showing the pattern of swirling clouds.

### Hard and soft Earth
The Earth is made up mainly of rock. On the outside is hard rock, forming a thin layer called the crust. Underneath is a thick layer of warm, softer rock, which makes up the mantle. The inner and outer cores are made up mainly of iron.

### Surface of Venus
We now know what the surface of Venus is like. Space probes have used radar beams to "look" through the clouds. The surface is covered with many craters. There are just a few highland areas.

### FACT BOX

• The temperatures on the planets Mercury and Venus are high enough to melt lead and other metals.

• The clouds in Venus's atmosphere are made of sulfuric acid.

• The crust of the Earth is only about 5 miles (8 km) thick in places.

• Oceans cover more than two-thirds of the Earth's surface.

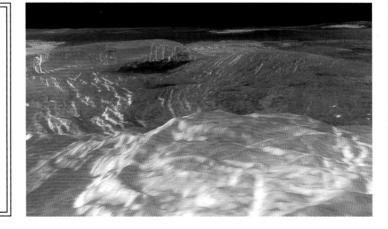

# ALL FALL DOWN

*Hundreds of miles (km) above Earth, an astronaut floats in space. The astronaut is weightless, but gravity still tugs at his or her body.*

WHEN you drop something, it falls. Something, therefore, must be pulling it down. That something is the Earth. We call the Earth's pull gravity. The Sun and all other planets have gravity, too. The Sun's gravity pulls at all the planets and keeps them in place in the solar system. But, back on Earth, if you drop a light object and a heavy object, which one hits the ground first? Common sense tells us that it must be the heavy object. But is this true? Carry out this experiment and find out. An Italian scientist named Galileo Galilei (1564–1642) is supposed to have carried out a similar experiment by dropping cannonballs from the top of the Leaning Tower of Pisa.

## Testing gravity

1 Paint one container gray to represent heaviness. Paint one container blue to represent lightness.

2 Fill the gray container with sand. Leave the blue one empty. Cover both containers with foil, taped down firmly.

3 Standing on a table, hold one container in each hand, and drop them at the same time. Ask a friend which container hits the ground first.

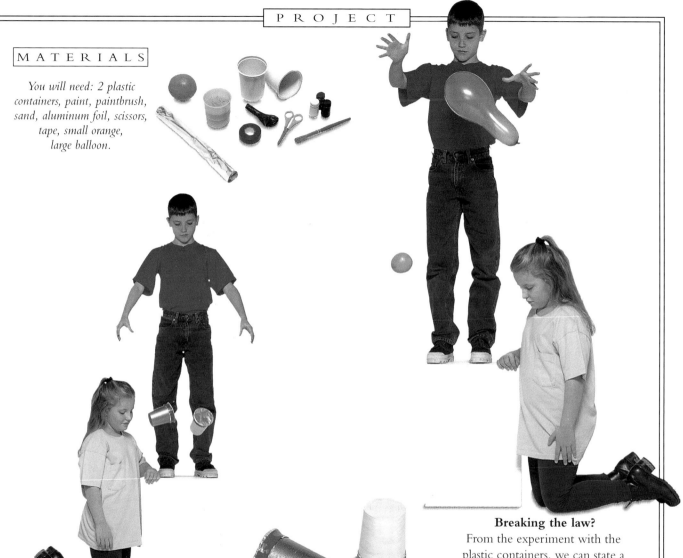

*You will need: 2 plastic containers, paint, paintbrush, sand, aluminum foil, scissors, tape, small orange, large balloon.*

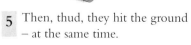

**4** Here are the two containers falling. They start together. Half-way down, they still are neck-and-neck.

**5** Then, thud, they hit the ground – at the same time.

**Breaking the law?**
From the experiment with the plastic containers, we can state a scientific law — falling bodies fall to Earth at the same rate. Now, carry out the same experiment using a small orange and a large balloon. Do they both hit the ground at the same time? If they do not, can you think why they do not?

# MARS AND MINI-PLANETS

The surface of Mars is a rusty brown color. The flat plains are covered with a sandy kind of soil and are littered with rocks.

Mars is another rocky planet like the Earth, but it is much smaller and has hardly any atmosphere. Temperatures on Mars do not often rise above the freezing point, even in the Martian summer. Several space probes, such as *Viking*, have visited the planet. In 1997, some cellular residue was discovered on Mars. Scientists are studying the residue to determine its origin. The space probes have also revealed some spectacular features on Mars, including a "Grand Canyon" and ancient volcanoes bigger than any that have been found on Earth.

Mars

Earth

Mars is a little over half the distance across as the Earth.

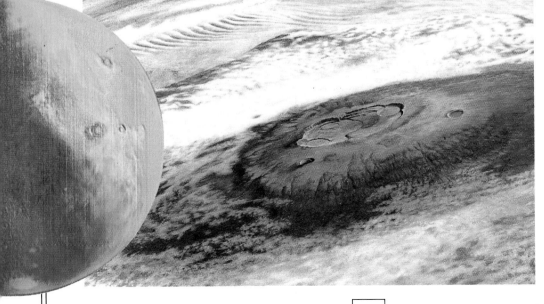

**Volcanic Mars**

Several huge ancient volcanoes have been found on Mars. They can be seen in photographs taken from space. They appear as circles in the false-color photograph taken by a *Viking* probe (*far left*). The biggest volcano (*left*) is known as Olympus Mons. It towers to a height of 16 miles (26 km).

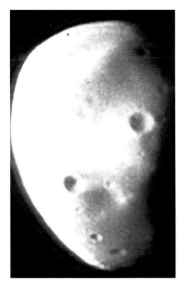

This is one of the two moons of Mars, called Deimos. It measures about 12 miles (19 km) across.

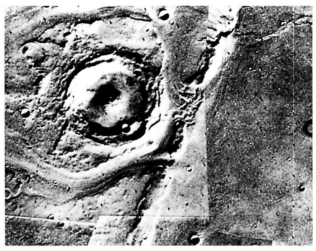

The two Viking *space probes were sent to map the surface of Mars beginning in 1976. They each split into two parts. One went into orbit and the other landed. The orbiters showed areas covered with craters and canyons* (above). *This picture* (right) *shows part of one of the landers.*

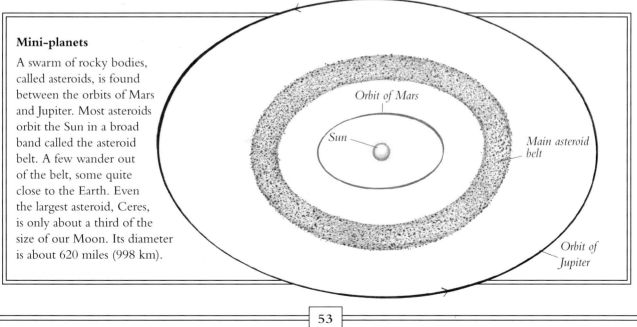

**Mini-planets**

A swarm of rocky bodies, called asteroids, is found between the orbits of Mars and Jupiter. Most asteroids orbit the Sun in a broad band called the asteroid belt. A few wander out of the belt, some quite close to the Earth. Even the largest asteroid, Ceres, is only about a third of the size of our Moon. Its diameter is about 620 miles (998 km).

Orbit of Mars

Sun

Main asteroid belt

Orbit of Jupiter

# JUPITER, THE GIANT

JUPITER is, by far, the biggest planet. To compare it with Earth, imagine Jupiter as a tennis ball and Earth as a pea. Jupiter is one of the so-called giant planets, which are made up in a different way from Earth. Jupiter has a tiny ball of rock at the center. Above this come layers of hydrogen in different forms – as a kind of metal, as a liquid, and as a gas in the atmosphere. When we look at Jupiter in telescopes, we see colored bands in the atmosphere. They are clouds that have been drawn out into bands as the planet spins around rapidly.

*Earth*

*Liquid hydrogen*

*Hydrogen gas atmosphere*

*Liquid hydrogen "metal"*

*Rock*

*Hydrogen gas atmosphere*

*Jupiter measures more than 87,000 miles (140,000 km) across. It is made up mainly of hydrogen in the form of a gas and a liquid.*

## Colorful Jupiter

Jupiter is one of the most colorful planets. Among its many moons is Europa *(right)*. The colorful bands you see in Jupiter's atmosphere are fast-moving clouds. The spots you can see are intense storms.

## Big moons

Ganymede and Io are two of Jupiter's four big moons. Here *(right)*, they are compared in size with the Earth's Moon. But they are different from the Moon. They contain a lot of ice as well as rock.

*Ganymede has a diameter of nearly 3,300 miles (5,300 km). It is the biggest moon in the solar system.*

## Spot on Jupiter

The most famous feature of Jupiter is the Great Red Spot. It is a huge storm of furiously whirling winds. This picture has been printed in false colors to show the patterns of clouds swirling around.

*Earth's Moon*

*Io is brightly colored because it is covered with sulfur. The sulfur comes from volcanoes.*

---

### FACT BOX

• Jupiter has no solid surface. Beneath its clouds is a deep ocean of liquid hydrogen.

• A day on Jupiter is less than 10 hours long.

• Jupiter has at least 16 moons. The biggest, Ganymede, is larger than the planet Mercury.

• Jupiter has a ring around it, but it is too faint to be seen from the Earth.

---

## One of Jupiter's moons

In close-up photographs, Callisto has a fascinating surface. There are dark regions and light ones with patterns of grooves. Tiny craters are everywhere, many ringed with ice.

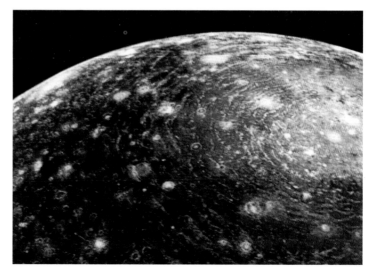

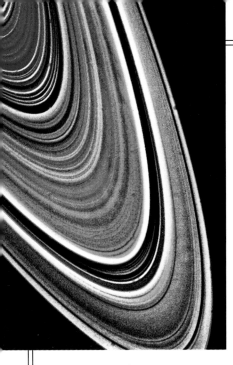

# MORE GIANTS

Saturn, Uranus, and Neptune are the three other giant planets that are made up largely of gases. All three have systems of rings around them, but only Saturn's rings can be seen easily from Earth. They are one of the wonders of the solar system. Like Jupiter, these other giants have many moons – Saturn has at least 22, Uranus at least 15, and Neptune at least eight. Uranus and Neptune cannot be seen with the naked eye from Earth. Uranus was not discovered until 1781 and Neptune not until 1846. The ninth planet, Pluto, was not discovered until 1930, but it is not a giant. It is a tiny body much smaller than Earth's Moon. Strangely, it has a moon that is half its size, which is relatively big for a moon.

*The many ringlets in Saturn's rings show up in this false-color picture. The different colors show that the ringlets are made of particles of different sizes.*

*This is Titan, Saturn's largest moon. It is the only moon we know that has a thick atmosphere.*

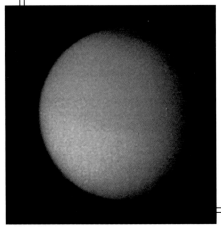

**Bright rings**

The *Voyager 2* space probe took this beautiful picture of Saturn from a distance of about 25 million miles (40 million km). Two bright rings can be seen, separated by a gap. Saturn has at least 22 moons. You can see two of them in the picture. One of them is casting a shadow on the planet.

## Distant Uranus

Uranus lies so far away that it takes 84 years to circle the Sun. Like all the other planets, Uranus spins around as it travels in its orbit. But, unlike all the other planets, Uranus spins on its side as it travels. The other planets spin around in a more or less upright position, like a top, as they travel along their orbits.

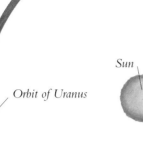

*Orbit of Uranus*

*Sun*

*Uranus*

*Triton, Neptune's largest moon, has a surface covered in snow and ice. Here and there, geysers shoot cold gases high above the surface.*

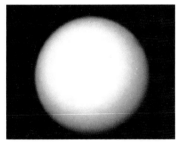

## Blue Uranus

Uranus has a thick atmosphere with a bluish color. The atmosphere covers a deep ocean of water and gases. We cannot see any clouds or storms in the atmosphere in the way that we see them on Jupiter and Saturn.

## Blue Neptune

Neptune, Uranus's twin, is another blue planet, but, unlike Uranus, it has some interesting features. There are patches of white cloud and dark oval regions. The biggest, shown here, is called the Great Dark Spot.

### TINY PLUTO

*Pluto*

*Earth*

The ninth planet in the solar system, Pluto, has a diameter of about 1,500 miles (2,400 km). It is even smaller than the Moon. We know little about Pluto. We cannot see it very well with telescopes because it is so small and so far away. Space probes have not visited it yet, but it almost certainly is made of water, ice, frozen gases, and some rock.

# METEORS AND COMETS

*This unusual photograph shows a meteorite breaking up as it plunges through the atmosphere. The small pieces will burn to ash, but the bigger ones might reach the ground.*

SOMETIMES, when you are stargazing, you see a streak of light in the sky that looks like a star falling down. A falling star, or a shooting star, is actually a meteor. A meteor is a piece of rock from outer space that burns up as it travels through the atmosphere. If it is big enough, it might reach the ground. Then we call it a meteorite. Large meteorites can make big craters. There are a few large meteorite craters on the Earth, and there are many on the Moon and on other bodies in the solar system. Most of the pieces of rock that form meteors have come from passing comets. Comets are great lumps of icy rock that appear in our skies from time to time. They gradually break up into dust and gas and glow in the sunlight. Some break up over thousands of years. Bright comets are a magnificent spectacle.

*Meteorites helped shape Saturn's moon Enceladus.*

### Dinosaur bones
Some scientists believe that the dinosaurs died out when a huge meteorite struck the Earth. They think the dust it kicked up blotted out the Sun, killing the plants on which the dinosaurs lived.

### Hole in the desert
The Arizona Meteor Crater is located in the Arizona Desert. A huge meteorite made the crater when it fell to Earth about 25,000 years ago. The crater measures nearly 4,300 feet (1,300 m) across and 575 feet (175 m) deep.

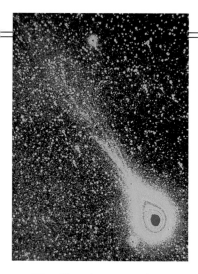

This false-color picture of a comet shows differences in brightness. The region in the center of the comet's head (red) is brightest. The tail (blue) is quite faint.

### Returning comet

A comet appeared at the time of the Battle of Hastings in 1066. It was recorded on the Bayeux Tapestry. Comets were thought to bring bad luck. This proved true for the English King Harold, who was killed. The comet that appeared in 1066 returns to our skies about every 76 years. It now is called Halley's Comet after Edmond Halley, who was the first to realize it was a regular visitor.

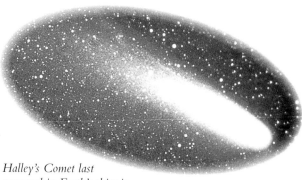

Halley's Comet last appeared in Earth's skies in 1986. It will not be seen again until 2062.

### Comet's tail

A comet grows a tail when it gets near the Sun. The tail is made of gas and dust, which reflect sunlight. The "pressure" of particles coming from the Sun pushes the gas and dust away from the comet's head to form a tail. Notice that the tail of the comet always points away from the Sun.

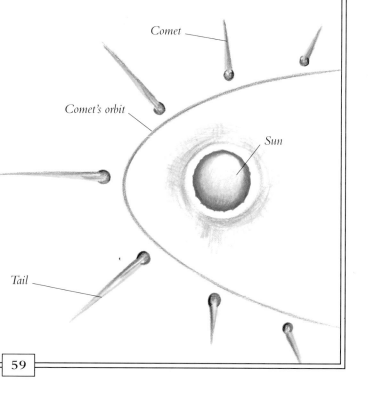

# ASTRONOMERS AT WORK

ASTRONOMERS study the stars with their eyes, binoculars, telescopes, radio receivers, electronic sensors, and other equipment. They work in places called observatories. Most observatories are located at a high altitude in a dry climate. There, they are above the thickest and dirtiest part of the atmosphere. In a dry climate, there is less moisture in the air and less chance for clouds. Telescopes are the main instruments astronomers use. The Italian astronomer Galileo Galilei first studied the heavens through a telescope in about 1609. He used a telescope in which glass lenses gathered and focused the light. This kind of telescope is called a refractor. Most astronomers today use telescopes in which mirrors gather and focus the light. These are called reflectors. Some have mirrors up to 20 feet (6 m) across.

*An amateur astronomer uses a reflecting telescope for serious stargazing. Mirrors gather and focus the light and reflect an image into the eyepiece for viewing.*

**Top of the world**
Kitt Peak Observatory (*above*) is one of the world's finest observatories. It occupies a mountain site in the Arizona Desert. The domes house large reflecting telescopes. Modern telescopes (*left*) have a skeleton frame for lightness.

## Pictures from space

Astronomers use big telescopes as cameras. They expose the film for long periods, so that the faint light from distant stars and galaxies builds up to give a brighter image *(above)*.

### Powerful telescope

The Hubble Space Telescope *(right)* is the most powerful telescope in space. The pictures it sends back show much more detail than pictures taken from big telescopes on the ground.

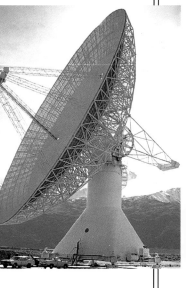

*The Hubble Space Telescope took this picture of the heart of a distant galaxy, with gas clouds and globular clusters (left). Telescopes on the ground show the galaxy as a white blob.*

### Satellites

Astronomers use satellites to carry instruments into space. The satellite *IRAS* looked at the heavens using invisible infrared light. It spotted great clouds of gases among the stars in the constellation Orion *(left)*. The star marked alpha (*a*) in the picture is one of the biggest stars we know, the supergiant Betelgeuse.

ROSETTA NEBULA

ORION

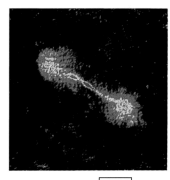

*A radio picture of a distant galaxy (right). It was made by using a computer to process the radio waves that the galaxy gives out.*

*Radio telescopes collect the radio waves stars and galaxies give out. This one (right) is located at Owens Valley in California.*

# MAKING A TELESCOPE

In their observatories, astronomers look at the night sky with reflectors – telescopes with mirrors. But these are difficult to make. Here, we show you how to make a refractor – a telescope with glass lenses. You cannot use just any lenses. You need to buy special ones from a hobby shop. Ask for one lens with a long focal length, about 12 inches (30 centimeters), for the objective lens and one with a short focal length, about 2 inches (5 cm), for the eyepiece.

*An experienced astronomer explains to a young one how a reflector works.*

### MATERIALS

*You will need: lenses, cardboard tube, adhesive, stiff black paper, tape, scissors, stickers.*

*An astronomer looks through a large refractor. This one has a main lens 27 inches (69 cm) across.*

## Make your own refractor

1 Attach the objective lens to one end of the cardboard tube with adhesive.

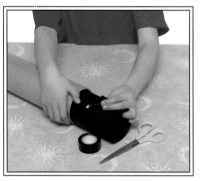

2 Roll the black paper into a tube shape so that it fits inside the other end of the cardboard tube.

3 Adjust the width of the paper tube to fit the eyepiece lens. Then attach the eyepiece lens with tape.

## Objective and eyepiece

On a refracting telescope *(right)*, the end lens of the telescope (the objective lens) gathers the light from the stars and forms an image, or picture. You view the image with a lens near the eye (the eyepiece lens).

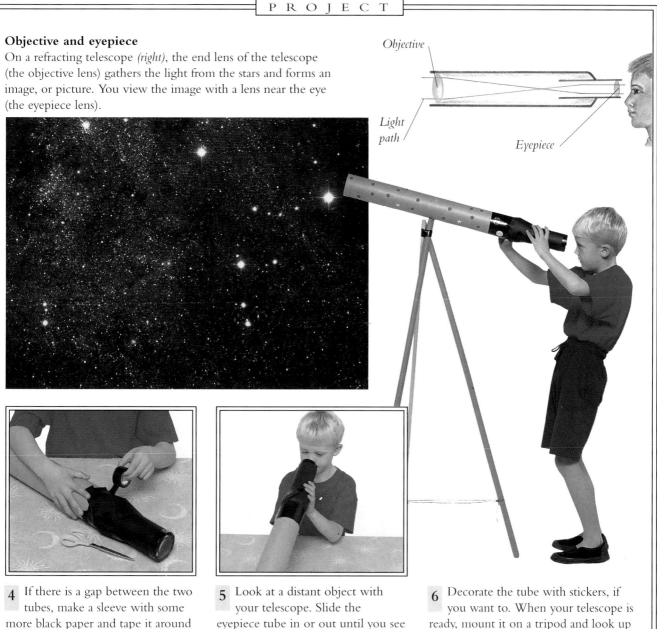

*Objective*

*Light path*

*Eyepiece*

**4** If there is a gap between the two tubes, make a sleeve with some more black paper and tape it around the gap.

**5** Look at a distant object with your telescope. Slide the eyepiece tube in or out until you see a sharp image. If necessary, adjust the lengths of the telescope tubes.

**6** Decorate the tube with stickers, if you want to. When your telescope is ready, mount it on a tripod and look up at the stars. You can make a tripod out of broom handles (see page 7).

# GLOSSARY

**asteroid** – a small, planet-like body that revolves around the Sun, usually between the orbits of Mars and Jupiter.

**astrolabe** – an ancient astronomical instrument used by early astronomers to observe the positions of the Sun, stars, and other heavenly bodies.

**astrology** – the study of the power that stars (especially those in the constellations) and other heavenly bodies may have on human beings.

**astronomer** – a person who studies astronomy.

**astronomy** – the study of the universe beyond Earth's atmosphere.

**atmosphere** – the air and gases surrounding the Earth, other planets, and other heavenly bodies.

**aurora** – streams of light in the upper atmosphere at the Earth's polar regions.

**Big Bang** – a theory in astronomy that the universe began with a huge explosion of gases 15-20 billion years ago.

**celestial equator** – the great circle on the celestial sphere, like the Earth's equator, where the northern and southern parts of the sphere (the hemispheres) come together.

**cluster** – a large group of hundreds or thousands of stars that travel together through space.

**comet** – a heavenly body that is like an icy lump made of gases and water that moves around the Sun and can be seen in our skies when its dust and gas glow in the sunlight.

**constellation** – a group of bright stars fixed in a shape or pattern that can be used to navigate through the night sky.

**corona** – a circle of light around a sun, moon, or other shining heavenly body. The outer atmosphere of the Sun is called a corona.

**eclipse** – a darkening of the Moon or the Sun when the Earth comes between the Sun and the Moon (lunar eclipse) or the Moon comes between the Earth and the Sun (solar eclipse).

**galaxy** – a huge system of stars held together by gravity in a region of space surrounded by empty space.

**gnomon** – (pronounced *NO-men*) the part of a sundial that sticks out from the center to cast a shadow on the scale marking the time of day.

**gravity** – the invisible force that pulls objects toward the center of the Earth and keeps all the elements of the solar system in place.

**latitude** – a certain distance either north or south of the equator that is measured in degrees of that location's angle with the North or South pole.

**light-year** – the distance that light travels in a year, which is almost 5.9 trillion miles (9.5 trillion kilometers).

**maria** – dusty plains, called seas, on the surface of the Moon.

**meteor** – a piece of rock from outer space that burns up as it travels through Earth's atmosphere.

**nebula** – a big cloud of gases and dust that is illuminated in the night sky by the stars around or behind it.

**observatory** – a building, usually located at a high altitude in a dry climate, that has the instruments and other equipment astronomers need to study the heavens.

**orbit** – the circular or curved path taken by a planet or satellite as it moves around and around another heavenly body.

**penumbra** – a partial shadow formed by the Moon or the Earth in a partial solar or lunar eclipse.

**photosynthesis** – a process in which green plants use the Sun's energy to convert carbon dioxide and water into sugar.

**planisphere** – a chart of part of the celestial sphere on a flat disk with another adjustable disk on top of it to show stars visible in the sky at a certain time and in a certain place on Earth.

**prominence** – a fountain of fire that rises thousands of miles (kilometers) above the surface of the Sun.

**red giant** – a big, bright star that does not burn as hot as some other stars and is much bigger in diameter than the Sun (which astronomers call a dwarf star).

**reflector** – a telescope through which objects are observed using mirrors.

**refractor** – a telescope through which objects are observed using glass lenses.

**satellite** – a small heavenly body that moves around a larger one in an orbit, like the Moon moving around the Earth. Also, a piece of equipment launched from Earth to study outer space.

**star map** – a chart that shows the patterns and positions of the stars.

**sundial** – an instrument that uses a shadow cast by the Sun to show the time of day on a scale of hours that is marked on its dial.

**supergiant** – a huge star that is thousands of times bigger and brighter than the Sun.

**umbra** – a complete shadow formed by the Moon or the Earth in a total solar or lunar eclipse.

**universe** – planets, moons, stars, nebulas, galaxies – everything that exists throughout space, including empty space.

**zodiac** – the imaginary path taken by the planets, the Moon, and the Sun through space each year, which is divided into twelve equal parts named after constellations.

# BOOKS

*Discover Stars and Planets.* Toni Eugene (Forest House)

*Discovering the Planets.* Jacqueline Mitton (Troll Communications)

*The Greatest Show Off Earth.* Margaret Mahy (Viking Children's Books)

*The Illustrated World of Space.* Susan Wells (Simon & Schuster Children's)

*Isaac Asimov's New Library of the Universe (series).* Isaac Asimov (Gareth Stevens)

*The Moon.* Michael George (Child's World)

*The Night Sky.* Peter Lafferty (Marshall Cavendish)

*Seeing Stars: A Book and Poster about the Constellations.* Barbara Seiger (Putnam Publishing Group)

*The Solar System.* Maura M. Gouck (Child's World)

*Solar System: Facts and Exploration.* Gregory L. Vogt (TFC Books)

*Space.* Carole Scott (Watts)

*The Space Atlas: A Pictorial Guide to Our Universe.* Heather Couper and Nigel Henbest (Harcourt Brace)

*Stars, Clusters, and Galaxies.* John R. Gustafson (Silver Burdett)

# VIDEOS

*Astronomy 101: A Beginner's Guide to the Night Sky.* (Mazon Productions, Inc.)

*How Many Stars.* (Pyramid Media)

*Introducing Astronomy.* (Society for Visual Education, Inc.)

*Isaac Asimov's New Library of the Universe (series).* (Gareth Stevens)

*The Moon; Outer Space.* (Disney Educational Productions)

*The Solar System.* (ESP)

# WEB SITES

seds.lpl.arizona.edu/billa/tnp/                    starchild.gsfc.nasa.gov/

Some web sites stay current longer than others. For further web sites, use your search engines to locate the following topics: *comets, constellations, galaxies, meteors, the moon, planets, solar system, and stars.*

# INDEX

## PICTURE CREDITS

b=bottom, t=top, c=center, l=left, r=right

Spacecharts/Royal Astronomical Society Library: page 4l. Spacecharts: pages 5tl, tr; 11tr; 22tl; 24bl; 25; 26t, cl, cr, bl, br; 28tr; 29tr, br; 38tr, bl, cb; 39tl, tr; 40tl; 43tr, tl; 48tl, bc; 49rb; 50tl; 52tl, bl; 53tl, tr; 54rb; 55tr, bl; 56tl, bl; 57tr, c, bl; 58tl; 59tl,tr,cl; 60tl, cr, bl; 61tr, tl, cr, bl, cb, br. Robin Kerrod: pages 5tl, br; 8bl; 10tr; 11bl; 34; 35; 43. NASA: page 58cr. Natural History Museum: page 58bl.